THE TRIBUTE HORSE

THE TRIBUTE HORSE

BRANDON SOM

WINNER OF THE 2012 NIGHTBOAT POETRY PRIZE

NIGHTBOAT BOOKS

BROOKLYN & CALLICOON • NEW YORK

© 2014 BY BRANDON SOM

SECOND PRINTING, 2019

ALL RIGHTS RESERVED
PRINTED IN THE UNITED STATES
ISBN: 978-1937658182

DESIGN AND TYPESETTING BY JASON BACASA
TEXT SET IN CASLON
COVER ART BY JANELLE IGLESIAS

CATALOGING-IN-PUBLICATION DATA IS AVAILABLE
FROM THE LIBRARY OF CONGRESS

NIGHTBOAT BOOKS
BROOKLYN & CALLICOON, NY
WWW.NIGHTBOAT.ORG

THE TRIBUTE HORSE

PREFACE

Brandon Som's collection *The Tribute Horse* opens with a meditation on his grandfather's name, which is also his own, Som. Beginning with this sound and its "stowaway vowel" Som begins exploring the history of his family, their language and their border-crossing as a way, perhaps, of repaying this "debt of sound."

He begins with the "coaching papers," the packet of papers immigrants carried with them to get them through the immigration process, including language cribs and other practical advice. In Som's case, the sequence of poems explore in deceptively simple language, a complex process of cultural transformations. "Breath to blood, breath fathomed me," he writes amidst other alliterative lines, the majority of which are comprised of monosyllabic words though sonically layered: "I sift spindrift for sound's wave."

In the poems that follow, Som continues to explore the ways that bodies cross boundaries—the zone between the known and the unknown for one kind, or planet-wide bodies of water like the Pacific Ocean for another. In *The Tribute Horse* they transmute, transform, becoming something other than what they are. Som's book explores all the ways migration acts upon a body's language, culture, perception and physical manifestation. Using found text, fractured lyric, prose poems and oulipian narrative, Som constructs a poetry deep in its theoretical rigor, ravishing in its sonic pleasure, and delicate in its formal constructions.

Drawing from various sources including Chinese painting, Japanese photography and the narratives of immigrants passing through Angel Island, Brandon Som channels the "drunk wren between me and dawn/ expert far flung tongue" and by so doing he is able to "forestall the fading path" and "burrow straight through song."

— *Kazim Ali*

for my family

ELEGY

My grandfather's grave in scorched grass has two names in the gravestone's granite: one with strokes—silent and once forbidden; the other lettered—a stowaway vowel between one aspirate, one liquid. Speech wears the written in the speaker's absence to stay the sound & breath's passing. I read that the wood, for Thoreau, was resonator Sundays when towns tolled bells— *Lincoln, Acton, Bedford, or Concord.* Pines with resin reverbed in sap what wind sent. A Chinese immigrant, on his Pacific-crossing, carried coaching papers for the memorizing. Approaching the island station, these pages were tossed to sea. A moon's light in a ship's wake might make a similar papertrail. My grandfather, aboard at twelve, practiced a paper-name. What ensued was a debt of sound.

COACHING PAPERS

Said, my name was a seine net,
torqued by pitch & drawn closed.

Said aloud, my name swallowed me.
Aloud, my name kept me in its net.

Nights, I hauled the wet nets: names
silent & breathless across my desk.

Nights, I mended trawling-tears.
I took needle & thread to names.

A paper-name ensures a debt
of sound. A paper wake, a ream

ripsawed by utter-breath, feathers
—tract to vane—my throat. I tamp,

binder (minding catchword order)
pages of crest-to-trough cursive,

a moon's sentence, a bow's hull-lap
beneath a farm boy's footstep.

The sea types in italics voices
analogged in the archive: soundbytes

shipsank or shore tossed—babble
for the gleaner. Bowsprit with tin-ear,

I dove & scissored a broomtail
long as the breath my lungs held,

long as the vow vesseling vowel.
Breath to blood, breath fathomed me.

At sea, paper turns to slurry.
The pulp's knit slips in the eddy.

Above are bareknuckled stars:
Hercules' keystone, Archer's teapot.

The sea calms & flatlines a blank.
Sign here or breach & breathe.

Fiddle slack the mute knot.
I sift spindrift for sound's wave.

Each sound—trill or siren,
grain-snap of apple, a woodfire—

earbones tap out from air
to sea wave. The ear's shape

cites physics: the lobe tableau
to a stone's throw—round, smooth

for the skip that left the ear wake—
rings where the stone sank.

At sea, a boy recites a name.
The sea records it in waves.

Som—aspirate, vowel, liquid—
is a vessel of wind & water.

On swells, the bow dips & rises
like a pen signing the horizon.

Som—aspirate, vowel, liquid.
There is a sea on the coaching pages.

The first page was lint left
after sifting & drying clothes

washed in a river whose length
stretched so far some claimed

the Milky Way for its source.
A laundry boy when he first

came over, father said of his
father trying to make a dollar.

Other sources cite hivemakers.
With its wood-grain mâché,

pulp & slur, a wasp masons—
utters what it gnaws, walls its say.

All good nests recite their trees.
Crack a hive's hymnal & read

the spackle's small mouth-print.
Write in that echo, that alphabet.

Breath vets veins, pleaches
bones, braids hairpin turns

in the well-dark body. I breathe
in loops, repeats, go to trees—

air between, ornithology. In slip
cuttings—beak-sown, spit-bound—

breath nests the sapling's coax,
when sounding the body's bones.

The *g*, singing to signing, falls
silent. You listen but it's you

breathing. To say *sea* we speak
first an aspirate. Wind starts a sea.

A ship's bow's shape writes an *A*
to mark the indefinite way. A name

is a persona, per son, per song.
Sonar searches the sea by singing.

The sea salts away a semblance
of the names in its sibilance.

Wading wavebreak or hunting
wrackline, we are in earshot

of the sea reciting. Nearing port,
the sea is a rehearsing of names

but shore-torn & reassembled
into unnamed sound & syllable.

A name goes searching for breath
aligning the sextant of its shape

with the plane of the written page.
I am charting a written name,

reading aloud a manifest of sons
marked Citizen, reciting to sound

out again the purchased names,
to hear what silence stowed away.

THE NEST COLLECTORS

Then the circuit tripped, and under alley stars
above the breaker box, I found the twig nest
with bits of hatchling shell. I considered the one-
note hum one's home makes, the murmur
of watt and want the nestlings fledged above,
forming their own warble from need-cry. Once
at a wedding's banquet, my father, so often frugal,
spoke on the extravagance of the first course,
of the trellises, in sea caves in China, centuries-old
and twine-tethered by nest collectors. Shouldering
gunnysacks damp with spindrift, they forage
swift nests for blood-spittle that binds twig
to twig and is a delicacy seasoning a soup's broth.
I looked for what bound my nest but found
nothing for profit, or to pawn, though in my hand
it was round as a pocketwatch—a pocketwatch
with fob that once tethered a bird. Mason of the avian,
father said, sipping from his Seven and Seven.
Then the sea bass came with slivers of scallion.
We used our soup bowls, discreetly, for the bones.

SEASCAPES

Of the horizon we know
Very little up close and figure
The intent as a streamlining
Of our own inarticulate selves.
Recently, I had the opportunity
To hold one in my hands. Let me
Underscore its resistance to form.
My fingers felt as if thousands
Of miles were between them.

Then they moved to the sea.
At the beach they let go
The kite string and the sky
Before them seemed even more
Immense and yet still
Leaning on those instances
That added up to the present
Sackcloth of clouds and wind
Assailing, suddenly all shoulders.

The story of the bird is a girl
In a devout grief against a sea
That eddies because its memory
Of the sky is at once collective
And dissipating as it becomes
Sky again. The plan was simple:
Fathom both grief and sea
With stones displacing each
The way a wing does the wind.

Underground disorients us
From above which explains why
We've forgotten so much of heaven.
A subway car sounds like you
Searching the silverware
For a tablespoon, while tunnels turn
The windows of the train to mirrors
Because the opaque, in its refusing
Of the light, affords us reflection.

They say in certain shells
You still hear the sea.
What urgency is there still
Left in such long distant
Phone calls in which the past
Is in our hands by some
Rendering tinged with loss:
The sea in desperate karaoke
Disarmingly maudlin in mono.

After this, bridges followed him
Home, shirking responsibility, so
The city was hamstrung. Telling him
Similar dreams of sawing men
In half, they approached the sympathies
That have made them the outbursts
Of our solitudes. Seeing something
Of himself, he watched them return
To tender themselves at dawn.

The essential idiom of the sea
Comes to terms in the calligraphic
Coast. Sea brought, kelp dries
In the sunlight on the shore rocks.
Day is a hogtying, a stark light
Drying them out, so she fished
From her day bag a tin of bee balm.
And the tide had its slip knot
And the day moon its oar lock.

Overtime, my lips were a kite
Tied off at the back of my throat.
Hers were a beak evolved
From a diet of settling a score.
Godlike, the sea swallowed
For the sake of form. Awe occurs
When we can't measure certain
Distances, while our mouths open,
As to challenge with our own immensity.

Among the ideal forms
Complete and hung past the veils
And valences of the night's sky
He liked those which explained away
His finding the old answering
Machine with its tape still spooled
And cued: she'd be late. These nights
He put a book down. He walked away.
Ellipses trailed him to the other room.

ALBA: THE ARCHER YI

Because we are helpless in the affairs
of heaven, we place feathers on arrows.
By dowel, the nock's groove against
its bowstring, the arrow by bird's wing
by archer's sight, by aim, superimposing
what is in hand over what is distant,
we arrive at certain conclusions, the end
of this tale for example: after blight
and the consequent famine, nine of ten
suns fell as dark crows. Of the ways
it is told, there's the account of the emperor,
as the ninth sun lay writhing—dark blood
on dark feathers—placing his hand on
the archer's shoulder, so the slung bow
was lowered, a discretion, the story would
have us believe, that is, finally, this sun,
this light, still with its obsession to travel
while we go on living in its obstruction,
even now, this morning, your shoulder pale
as scrimshaw, drawing the light to its fletching.

ELEGY

Of Babel's moon, I have notes. It was a marked card. It lit a chandelier out of an acacia. The trowel glinted with it. Crickets were out too, and, as if they sightread stars, settled in to leg-kick song. A light wind blew seed into the web between tines of a hayrake. A soldier stood letting his horse drink well water from his helmet. The moon trembled in it. There was nothing forsaken about it. It simply issued a shadow while burnishing a surface. This morning, I read that when returning from a trail, Thoreau knew he had had visitors by what was left behind: *a wreath of evergreen, a name in pencil on a walnut leaf, a willow wand woven into a ring*. Its path not without disruption, the moon, in its orbit, tethers and tethers again. The morning of the funeral, my father dressed my grandfather: from the eyelet, each button, new to full; the tie's knot loose as if it had swallowed a small bird.

CUTTINGS

For proof,
prune the canes
& small twigs,

tending
a fluent light
path,
shearing

to satiate
the flowerhead.

For proof,
the turned
out tilma made

a bowl
for December
roses sown

in hill loam
above the desert
diocese.

Be bishop
& penitent
to the portrait—

what bled
thorn-told testimony

offset on
the neophyte's
coarse garment.

Kneel with me
in this light
& see the sepals
bent back

on blooms
like those about
their cassocks.

Make then
the cut clean
above

a five-
leaflet leaf
to prevent

disease & dieback
in the raw
stalk, & so

ensure new growth.

In the accounts I have read, there are never shears, not even a small blade.
Can one stem's thorn cut the stalks of other blooms? *Sever, riven*: words
with cuts within them. Did the Virgin offer something—a machete,
simple house scissors? Gardening manuals suggest cuts at an angle, & to
choose the buds just beginning to loosen. Both *knife* & *knowing* begin
in silence—what appears but does not say, the ghosts of ragged cuttings.
The tilma was a mantle made from the cut fibers of a maguey plant. The
Spanish for knife is *cuchillo*, the double *l* read *y*: a *yeoman's yoke*, a *yucca*—
that desert shrub some call Spanish bayonet. It is also known, in other
regions, as Adam's needle-and-thread.

TILDE

The twine tied about the bird's leg would some mornings still be wet from a neighbor's bath. In air & frayed, the twine streamed out from the twig-thin leg. In winter, the stone bath froze & kept a feather for itself. Saying *feather* will coax the tongue, that molted bird, to its cage. I stayed in & read for days—sometimes silent, sometimes aloud. With the dark letters smaller than a millet seed, I made all kinds of sound. Rains came. Soon, I found the banded bird in a hedge of jade. Cutting the knot loose, I noted the twine's tongue-shape, imagined it then in my mouth, gagging a bit on the filth—a nest's lice, a field's dung—the foreignness, the trespass of what it might say. *To return* in Spanish—volver—requires the tongue to buckle & rill. Think burble, think babble. Volume is a word we use to measure both sound & water. Was I wrong then to think each letter a liter? Or each page—página y pájaro—fastened & fraught with syllable? There were so many birds. How boyish, how foolish to follow just one.

A CROW'S ROBE

'A bridge of magpies'—long-tailed crows
whose caw-worked nest is collage, rich
with heist—joins the two: one, immortal,
who loomed heaven's vestments; the other
mortal, cattleman, a vaquero with clutch
of stars in his herder's head. & her gaze
on his herding upset patterns: a bobbin's
slip was a crooked hem. Audubon drew
grackles, *Quiscalus Quiscula*, in summer corn.
A team these two—dressed in shadows,
teasing hairs from husks—one watches, dark
pupil in white, while the other cocks back
craw for kernel. Perhaps they are kin to that
crow found in *The Classic of Mountains & Seas*,
collecting shore stones for retribution. Once
an emperor's daughter, she drowned too far out
in rough waters, & feathered now, flies
intent on choking dry, stone by stone, an ocean.
A bay's breakwater, where boats huddle,
is a design of similar ambition & tragedy.
'I ate wind and tasted waves,' writes the poet
of his Pacific crossing. Ships then had
presidents' names: Pierce, Lincoln, McKinley.
Grandfather came in '28, a steamer berth,
S.S. Madison, to claim himself son of a citizen,
'a crooked path,' avoiding exclusion. In another tale,

dubious & apocryphal, I have come across
a robe entrusted to a beggar of Hunan Province
with powers to turn whomever wore it into a crow.
Of its design & material, nothing is written.

Before another rasp-worked moon, I'll tender a clutch of cardinals, or the flush on a runner's cheek to better render the young girl's gift to the Christ-child. Flame Leaf. Star Flower. What is evening in evening? By what accounting? The sky will go away despite the trees thrashing & the smoke giving chase from the chimneys. "Too much torn to make a drawing," Audubon wrote of a hermit thrush after the day's hunt. Isn't it also true of some stories? The infinite graftings. Here, you take a cutting. The blood-colored leaf, once over the heart, was thought to increase circulation. Ingested, it was believed to reduce fever. You might, however, place it in the pages of a breviary beside a favorite psalm.

BOWS & RESONATORS

1

A calabash gourd,

from an earthen mould, grown
russet
& rounded,

then fitted with a lid of jade,
once housed

a *golden bell*, a prized singer

popular with fanciers
in Peking
& the bazaars of Java,
its chime, heard warm nights,

said to strike
the same pitch as the small, sacred
handbells

of 'Shinto priestesses.'

Talk of the teashop,
fed on wormwood & radish,

this 'chorister' once

caught in bamboo trap-boxes
baited

with votive candles

had then each wing waxed to amplify
the song

resonant
in the gourd & rising out of
measured holes,

hollowed from the jade:

the eyes, nose, & claw of a dragon,
that revered go-between

of the terrestrial & the heavenly.

2

In the barrack wall at Angel Island—

'Grief
and bitterness
entwined are heaven sent.'

The moon appears,
though 'faintly,'
twice

      —as moon
& as 'sun and moon' for 'shine.'

The wind outside
is recorded

'faintly' also & 'whistling.'

The insects
beneath the moon
tether its line

      & 'chirp'

—sound & light,
like plucked strings both

vibrate.
The poem over time
was filled with putty, painted, written on
& painted

over again, some eight times.

The thinking was 'graffiti'
from the Italian *graffio*, 'a scratch.'

To invent writing,

'Ts'ang-Chieh, if certain ancient
books are to be believed,

observed the marks

of birds' claws
and animal's foot-prints upon the ground,

the shapes of shadows cast
by trees,

        ...and engraved...

their forms upon the sticks'

The barrack had timbered walls
from woods milled

in the Sierras, felled Sequoias—
those redwoods
named for the Cherokee scholar
who devised for his tribe

an alphabet.

            Muir in those groves—

Kaweah & Tule,
        Fresno & Mariposa,

Merced & Tuolumne,
       Calaveras & Stanislaus—

describes one tree,

'24 feet inside the bark,'
& thirteen hundred years old

cut down for its stump

       to be a dance floor.

3

Besprinkled, Bordeaux, mitred, stove,

black & yellow tree,
chicken of the weaver's shuttle, horse of the hearth,

watchman's rattle—

fiddlesticks: one rib hook
of teeth

bows against the other wing's

'rungs'

(flightless
wings have ladders)

over a resonator,
'four drums'

of taut skin, smoke-tint,
by which the cricket

in sod, sedge, hall, or hearth
'throws his music'

—& the bells: pagoda, flowered, golden, stony, & blue.

4

'Sound,' it has been written,

'exists
only when it is going out

of existence.'

Yet sound, traveling in waves,
was once thought
to never

go out completely

but to continue at shorter & shorter
frequency,

vibrating faintly. There waiting

on Angel Island,
             a poet recorded,

'The insects chirp outside the four walls.'

Carving the sound, the man
hews & whittles
closer

to the sound coming through,
those 'stridulations,'
from the Latin, 'a creaking.'

'Here the baldest symbol':

'each character composed within
an 'ideal square.'

To square the sound
the radical 'kou' in the left hand
corner,

a box-spelled warble, a box-made trill.

To its right
a grammatical character

translates variously,

so there is,
at the time of,
if, close, & to.

Twice-made, here in pinyin:

$$jî$$
$$jî$$

The standard system
of transliterating since the 1960s,

Pin-yin means
literally

    'spell-sound.'

Ezra Pound in his notes
to the writings of the Sinologist,

Fenollosa, tells us,

'...unfinished; I am proceeding

in ignorance
and by conjecture.

The primitive pictures were
'squared'

at a certain time.'

'The inmates,'

the poem in the wall
continues,

        'often sigh.'

5

The 'object of his bow'—

the grass music
that Thoreau wrote,

'annihilates time and space';

the 'neverend' Po Chu-i believed

of his sleepless night

during the Tang—

that period when the palace
women first kept
crickets

bedside in cages,

entreating song
with coos or 'leaf-lettuce.'

Fabre's 'hosanna' from
rosemary

in Provence
has us staring through
the 'veined pinion' of a Bordeaux,

which tints things slightly red.

Thoreau's 'elixir'—
'I see clear through,' he tells us,

'summer to autumn.'

6

Dolbear

to test a law,

walked out under stars
white & clustered,

as summer's
calf-high,
Queen Anne's lace

& listened

counting evensong,
like a prosody, on his fingers

to hear the heat & balm
in the chirr

& by logarithm
measure,
in Fahrenheit, the field.

Mic-ing the inner ear,
scientists have recorded the hairs

shook in seawash,

so we might hear what
hearing
sounds like: a night bug

abrading
wing-teeth

          —a field
of bulrush & burr,
a cappella

amid chicory,

all
sizzling like a pan steak.

7

Shell-shaped, & so traces

of sea, our ears have long been tuned
to pattern.

'A movement
of what can rebound,'
all sound,

according to Aristotle,
is already echo.

'Island' interrogators had translators,
interpreters
who knew dialects

& listened to catch

men quoting other men's lives
for their papers.
     'Sounds passing

through sudden rightnesses,'
voices sustain

spaces of resonance—

   'Sadly, I listen
   to the sounds of insects

   & angry surf.

   The harsh laws pile
   layer upon layer;

Rumor has it, Aristotle had a stammer.

He observed

a voice to be 'the impact of the
inbreathed against
the windpipe.'

Thus imagined, a voice requires walls
for the breath

'to knock.'

8

In the old tales,
the crisis often involves a prized

cricket's escape:

whether it's the rare, long-legged one
for which the minister
of state

trades his best horse, or the
undersized

fighter brought finally to fury
by the tickling

of a 'pig's whisker,'

or the favorite of the ruling
court—chestnut
in color,

& able to 'dance in time' to the languid
hum of eunuchs.

In the old tales,
there is often a seamstress
holding

a needle
& wanting you to lick the thread.

A travel-weary visitor appears

only to slough off
his skin
beside the 'rice-granaries'

& sing.

'I was in the field where memory first happened,'
one
narrator tells us,

that field that swallows
swords & is equally as intimate

with robins.

9

According to Pliny the Elder,

'if a man doe
but touch
the amygdals

or almonds of the throat,

with the hand
wherewith he hath bruised
or crushed

the said Criquet,
it will appease

the inflamation thereof.'

Likewise,

'...digged up
& applied
to the plase, earth
& all

where it lay,

is very good for the ears.'

OULIPO

So then me and you come
You assured led by the tongue
Dark fall a winding wind
A detour circles song

Drum din when the rain comes
Erasure the song sung
Details wandering in a wren
Ditto cuckoo song

Truth bends when you hum
Jig lure reel rig seine
Bird calls wander heavens
The fall circles round

Often we were conned
Trees were things wrens sung
Too tall wild in midair
Falsettos so soon hamstrung

Kerplunk plans mean you've come
Be sure these songs swim
Phonecall frogmen when
Tempos spiral down

Bunkbeds wing me across
Secure belonging's bobbin
Seawalls make waves mist
Tiptoe tidal flats

Trouble the sea for a son
Feel sure you don't belong
You don't write what men say
Sea tales consume song

Trundled nights of a nun
Fissures between rival tongs
You sell wontons here
Detuned doo-wop songs

Backhand within each psalm
Young girl in a tea-stained sarong
Make-do the long nightmare
Lingo miscues song

Just in sweet meat buns
Insure deeds with alms
Doorbells wane once you're in
Dark clouds sluice down shrubs

Strum then strings you've strung
Speech chirrs inside tongues
You sell wrong names here
Data research shows

Trunks fend off wind that comes
Leeward they have swung
So long waiting here
This talk cites coos wrong

A monk lends me his car
Bugs chirr sovereign songs
Clouds shawl a wan mien
A junco suitor calls

Drunk wren between me and dawn
Expert far-flung tongue
Forestall the fading path
Burrow straight through song

Translate dreams in sons
Be sure to tear shit up
Due to wagers made here
Pray tell absurd sounds

Dressed in tight ass funds
He sure street fought some
Shut out wrong men here
All told buckles song

Trumped again add up sums
Leave sure you've had your fun
Dutiful sons wandered here
Laid down bicycles in the sun

Locket syrinx in a palm
Procure mahjongg songs
Judo bygone rift rafts
Echoes pseudo song

CONFESSIONS

My watermarked mouth
    marsh mud
& bay silt
wrackline welt
     tongue like saltfish

Teeth seine
    & lips purse
make a meadow
of lost boats
     in eelgrass & sea lettuce

Harvested seabeds
    What was under
I was over or in
Sat in boat cabins
     with gill-sucking fish

Know well
    the wave cut shore
the hollows
what sea cannot swallow
     bay basin dregs

The undertows
   the moon tills
    o   *o*   *o*
disav w av w v w
pitch waves unutterable
    as I fish

      *

Rusted from the wet
   my rivet
Adam's apple
smelt from kettle handles
    cast clank & clang

Swallowed
   like a coke oven
Pig stubborn
pig iron
    made for little to say

Made the executioner
   sword sing
a smith's hammer
stammer
    to shake him to his teeth

Smith-made
  a larynx chinks
Words clamor
pan-chatter
    or sustain on steel string

May play my pulse
  ear
      to the rail
Betrayal
    still beats there

                    *

Thrown in
  & then rose out
trans-Pacific
of precedents
      cedar-like

Essence stretches
    tumescent
beach pea & sea-fig
See fig.
    11

stilts in sea silt

telos
Tell-tail
my queue availed
     to sea wind

Plumb lined
    thigh to shin
Fathomed
there abandoned
     to sea death

Sleepwalked after
    beside a boat-bottom
moon
miles grown
      between shoulders & shoes

       *

Can't tinder flame
    Kin but unkindled
Whelmed I wear it
livid
    yellow

Tied there to ignite
    in torch-lit wood

my body staked
forged fake
    a look-alike

By that light
    was a gilt-edged
page
bound displayed
    & given sentence

Char-grit
    the smoke left
was lampblack
to sign one
    duplicate

Flame both singular
    & effusive
can't tinder which
In et al. lynch
    who isn't yellow by fire

*

Long as starlight
    could kiss
or hold a note

No concern for bones
    swallowed whole

Thought breath
    that dive-bird lungbound
intimate
with what let
      me say my self

Thought exhales dealt
    in essence
spiritus
testing the bellow's glue
      how steam confesses kettles

Sentenced breathless
    kiln-locked
cap to capillaries
could not rat or canary-
      sing

Lungs heavy holding
    held my tongue
throat-long & air tied
alibi
      elsewhere

THE TRIBUTE HORSE

1

The handscroll woven from silk
has a finch in the cane rendered
in the ink of lampblack. Because
with some beauty you feel the need

to talk aloud to it, tell it about itself,
I got closer until I could see the depth
produced by the silk sucking on
the soot, & slightly self-conscious,

I addressed the bird, asked whether
it were sketched with a switch
of willow or a brush of goat's hair.
It was endeared & twittered there,

flit in the cane. It asked me if I were
the scholar or the angler, if I saw
the horsemen with the tribute horse
pass the village on the way to court.

2

Often ink-stones were roof-tiles,
clay wattle from imperial houses
with names like Bronze-Bird-Terrace.
What kept rain out, kept ink wet.

A brick of ink fledges—a bird
in the stroke settles on the strokes'
branches, lifts & leaves them
a metronome's sway. A hollow

stroke returns to smoke traces.
The dry brush returns & wets
its bristles in ground soot and gum
kept wet in the stone's well,

that house for the ink's dark.
Under roof is want & over,
a well's winch, a finch's chit,
light tappings sounding the depths.

3

If my song were smoke, I would knot
the braid & cut its movement upwards,
lariat the sinews, harnessing bone
to muscle the kite of the cane birds.

I would knot & bird the line as birds
notch the branch or leave steps
in bank mud. I would thieve the tracks
as I would the pine's shape as it shadowed

& stretched a figure past the furthest
branches' reach. Each tree shadows.
Each tree shades. Each tree thirsts
& traffics resin. What a pine darkens

foreshadows its pitch in the pine-smoke.
My song, if my song were smoke, would
rise from kindling & reach, pine-like,
past itself to where the wind takes it.

4

A calligrapher, in order to regain
the confidence of birds, selects
a whisker brush fringed with rabbit fur
& bundled with an ivory mount

on a handle hewn from bamboo.
The whisker is plucked from field mice
& the fur from the rabbit's flank
in autumn before its winter molt.

With thumb & forefinger, a bird's
beak at the wrist's service, he has
mastered his strokes—*bending
weed, sheep's leg, dropping dew.*

But it is a seed-eating bird he wants
in the stroke-work of the word,
the trill answer in the coarse rustle
of brush across the page grain.

5

Dear finch, that you may have fed
on the worm that if left to live
makes the silk thread, on which
—woven now—you, lighter

at the breast, darker on the wing,
flit and rest, poised for flight
out of the cane, suggests a weaving
finer than I might have guessed.

Legend says an empress found
in her tea a cocoon undone
by the water's heat, & wound
the thread around her finger.

Spinners need spools, dear finch.
Four sloughs & the worm weaves
a cocoon for wings. Seems you,
dear finch, have borrowed these.

The poem SEASCAPES works from the photographic series *Seascapes* by Hiroshi Sugimoto.

Sources for the poem BOWS & RESONATORS include the following: Mark Him Lai, Genny Lim, and Judy Yung, *Island: Poetry and History of Chinese Immigrants on Angel Island, 1910-1940*; Lisa Gail Ryan, *Insect Musicians & Cricket Champions: A Cultural History of Singing Insects in China and Japan*; Jean Henri Fabre, *Fabre's Book Of Insects;* Frank Cowan, *Curious Facts in the History of Insects*; Ernest Fenollosa (ed. Ezra Pound), *The Chinese Written Character as a Medium for Poetry*; Wallace Stevens, *The Collected Poems*; Walter J. Ong, *Orality and Literacy*; Steven Connor, *Sound and the Pathos of the Air*. Thanks to Nick Admussen for advisement with translation.

The quatrains in the poem OULIPO are homophonic translations of Li Po's "Night Thoughts," as recited by Lo Kung-Yuan in Peking dialect for the 1963 Folkways Record, *Chinese Poems of the Tang and Sung Dynasties*. Li Po's poem is also inscribed on the wall of Room 105 at the immigration station on Angel Island. Thanks to Amaranth Borsuk for help with the poem's title.

The poem CONFESSIONS is based on the 1938 American children's book *The Five Chinese Brothers* by Claire Huchet Bishop and Kurt Wiese.

THE TRIBUTE HORSE works from the painting *Finches and Bamboo* by the Song Emperor, Huizong, and is indebted to Chiang Yee's book *Chinese Painting*.

ACKNOWLEDGEMENTS

Grateful acknowledgement is made to the editors of the journals in which the following poems first appeared, sometimes in earlier versions:

SEASCAPES (originally titled SUGIMOTO): *Octopus Magazine*; A GOLDEN BELL (now the opening section of BOWS & RESONATORS), ELEGY: *Prism Review*.

The poem ALBA: THE ARCHER YI was chosen for the anthology *Best New Poets 2007* edited by Natasha Trethewey.

The poem THE NEST COLLECTORS was featured on the website *Poetry Daily*.

CUTTINGS, as well as sections of CONFESSIONS and BOWS & RESONATORS, will appear in the forthcoming anthology *Both and Neither: Biracial Writers in America*. Gracious thanks to the editors Brenda Shaughnessy and Monica McClure.

Several poems from this manuscript appear in the chapbook *Babel's Moon*. Gracious thanks to Aimee Nezhukumatathil and Tupelo Press for their selection of this chapbook for the 2009 Snowbound Series Chapbook Award.

For their guidance and commitment to this project, I would like to thank Kazim Ali and Stephen Motika at Nightboat Books.

Additional thanks to the Provincetown Fine Arts Work Center and the Virginia Center for the Creative Arts for fellowships that provided me time, space, and community in which to work.

For their inspiration and advisement, I would like to thank Susan McCabe, David St. John, Mark Irwin, Carol Muske-Dukes, John Carlos Rowe, Bruce Smith, and Marjorie Perloff.

And special thanks to Stacey Waite, Jason Bacasa, Stan Mir, Carolina Maugeri, Francine Harris, Dave and Jessica Griffith, Mike Bunn, Dave Carillo, Josh Rivkin, Solmaz Sharif, and Ari Banias for their friendship, encouragement, and insight.

ABOUT THE AUTHOR

BRANDON SOM is the author of the chapbook *Babel's Moon*, winner of the Tupelo Press Snowbound Prize. His poems have appeared in *Barrow Street*, *Indiana Review*, *Black Warrior Review*, and *Octopus Magazine*. He has received fellowships to the Virginia Center for the Creative Arts and the Provincetown Fine Arts Work Center. He currently teaches in the Literature Department at the University of California, San Diego.

NIGHTBOAT BOOKS, a nonprofit organization, seeks to develop audiences for writers whose work resists convention and transcends boundaries. We publish book rich with poignancy, intelligence, and risk. Please visit our website, www.nightboat.org, to learn about our titles and how you can support our future publications.

This book was made possible by grants from The Fund for Poetry and the Topanga Fund, which is dedicated to promoting the arts and literature of California.

The following individuals have supported the publication of this book. We thank them for their generosity and commitment to the mission of Nightboat Books: Elizabeth Motika and Benjamin Taylor.

In addition, this book has been made possible, in part, by a grant from the New York State Council on the Arts Literature Program.

State of the Arts

NYSCA